THE 23 COMMANDMENTS OF BRANDING

How to Build Brands that Bring You More Business!

JEROME C. FORD

The 23 Commandments of Branding

23 Ways to Grow Your Brand without Going Broke

I wrote this book for people who want to successfully brand their business without spending an arm and a leg.

The idea for the book came after 30 years of frustration. I've seen so many good hard-working people with great business ideas and plans fail miserably, because they didn't brand and market their business properly.

Very Few people know the secrets in this book because most of the information and so-called knowledge of branding is based on old school, outdated information.

Many branding and marketing experts don't know what I'm about to show you because they've been taught in schools with teachers that hide behind big words and lame theories instead of real-world responses and results.

You may wonder is this book for me? So let me ask you the following questions:

Do you want your brand to succeed?

Do you want to see a return on your investment?

Are you looking to make yourself or your brand famous?

Do you see yourself as your own Boss?

Do you want to help people who could use your expertise?

Do you have a great product or idea but don't know how to brand it?

Have people told you that what you do is amazing and you should get paid for it?

Have people said they would pay you, to do what you love to do?

Are you ready to make your business dreams a reality?

Are you ready to prove those who doubted you wrong?

Are you ready to move your brand to the next level?

Whatever your motivation The 23 Commandments of Branding will help you take your brand to the next level.

Copyright 2019-2031 Jerome Ford

Table of Contents

What is Branding? 8

Branding Commandment #1 Know Your Target Customer 13

Branding Commandment #2 You Must Make Great Impressions 18

Branding Commandment #3 Use Your Expertise and Authority .26

Branding Commandment #4 Hit them with the WIIFM! 27

Branding Commandment #5 Don't Forget the BIG BENEFIT 29

Branding Commandment #6 Never Confuse Features and Benefits 30

Branding Commandment #7 Tell Them Your Why 32

Branding Commandment #8 Sell that Sizzle 36

Branding Commandment #9 Sell Excitement 38

Branding Commandment #10 Make it Easy to do Business with You 39

Branding Commandment #11 Know when to use Logic and Emotions 41

Branding Commandment #12 Shake Them Up! 44

Branding Commandment #13 Use Reference Points 46

Branding Commandment #14 Appeal to Your Target's Pain 47

Branding Commandment #15 Make Your Message's Stick 49

Branding Commandment #16 Know How to Beat Your Competition 52

Branding Commandment #17: Create Copy that Converts 55

Branding Commandment #18: Avoid Big Words 58

Branding Commandment #19 Don't forget Your Call to Action! .59

Branding Commandment #20 Use a Swipe File 60

Branding Commandment #21 Brand to the Media You're Using .61

Branding Commandment #22 Use A/B Testing 62

Branding Commandment #23 Be Consistent 63

The Bad News is…

According to research by the Small Business Administration, Bloomberg and Forbes magazine, up to 8 out of 10 businesses fail within 18 months.

80% of Businesses (brands) Fail within 18 Months.

That's right, 8 out of 10 businesses fail within a year and a half!

Why do so many brands fail so fast?

Brands don't fail because of money – or lack thereof. Brands fail because the people in charge fail to brand and market the right way.

There's a myth out there that says it takes money to make money.

Many people believe that you need an angel investor, rich relative, a bank loan or huge amounts of cash to start and run successful business. This myth is not true.

There are many successful entrepreneurs who started with little to no money. Don't believe me? Check out this article (https://www.entrepreneur.com/article/231909).

The ugly truth is, it takes branding and marketing to make money and grow your business.

I've meet with hundreds of clients who have successfully branded their business. What I've seen working with winners and losers, is that there are 23 commandments of branding that EVERY BRAND owner must follow to keep brand in business.

The great thing is these 23 commandments – if not broken, will make branding your business easy and can skyrocket your business into success for years!

"80% of businesses fail *Because business owners fail to brand.*"

What do the businesses that beat the odds and succeed for years and in some cases, centuries do to succeed? The answer is simple. They use the secrets of branding.

In this eBook, you'll learn how the 20% of business owners use branding to defy the odds, prevent failure, and grow their businesses.

The 23 commandments of branding will show you how to successfully brand your business without going broke. No matter what sized budget you have, this book will teach you how to become a master of branding in no time.

The 23 commandments of branding are proven and based on years of behavioral economics, neural linguistic programming (NLP), marketing research, psychology trial, error, experience and most importantly, the successful outcomes of my clients.

These are the 23 must-know techniques for anyone trying to brand their business.

What is Branding?

"Branding is getting people to know about what you offer before they need or want what you offer"

Branding is the first stage of the marketing process. Branding is the act of getting your brand top of mind with your prospects *before* they decide to buy what they are going to buy.

In marketing terms, we call this Top of Funnel. There are 3 main stages to each marketing funnel; Top of Funnel, Middle of Funnel, and Bottom of Funnel.

The first stage is the Top of Funnel (awareness stage). This is where people get to know your brand and what it offers.

The second stage is the Middle of Funnel (consideration stage). This is where people think about doing business with you.

The third stage is the Bottom of Funnel (conversion stage). This is the most important stage. A conversion can be a website click, a follow or subscription on social media or the best of all sales of your products!

```
         Awareness

       Consideration

          nversi
```

So, What is "Branding"?

<u>Branding is the management of impressions</u> (more on impressions shortly).

A lot of people confuse branding and marketing. It's like confusing the tires on a vehicle with the steering wheel. There are similarities (they are both round, they are both needed to drive) but they are not the same.

"Branding begins before the sale.
Marketing begins during and after the sale".

These days the buzz word on social media is "brand" but there is way more to branding than just declaring you are a or have a "brand".

You must build your brand before people need or want the product or service you offer.

Working in mulita-media for the last 33 years, I've witnessed tragic stories of business owners borrowing up to hundreds of thousands of dollars to finance their brands, only to have those businesses fail shortly after opening because they failed to properly brand their business.

Many branding failures go like this: Someone invests time, money, and sometimes blood, sweat and tears into a business. These people sadly believe by having a Grand Opening, or launching their business online that people will say "oh there's a new business...I must go and spend my money with them".

Instead, sadly what usually happens is customers ignore the business and that business goes out of business.

Have you ever noticed a company advertising that their having a 'going out of business sale' and thought to yourself, I've never heard of them?

Tragically, many businesses don't take branding seriously until they are having their out of business sale.

That's because these people fail to understand or use the unbreakable commandments of branding.

Arron was the owner of a cell phone store in Grand Rapids, Michigan. Arron had a great location in a busy shopping center. He called Goodrich Media (the company I worked for) because he wanted to buy some advertising. I went to his store and there were no customers. Arron told me he was hoping that people would see his big window sign, be curious and come in the store.

I told Arron that he would need to do more to get people into his store. I suggested that Arron do some radio advertising. Arron said no and told me that he was going to do a "soft grand opening" and give away free hotdogs and soda. I shook Arron's hand and wished him the best.

Three months later, Arron called me back and said that he really needed a miracle. His soft grand opening only got him one customer. He spent hundreds of dollars buying food and drinks. Many people stopped in for the drinks, but no one ate the hotdogs and only one person signed up for a new phone. I told Arron there were people who needed new phones, but he wasn't reaching out to enough people.

I put Arron in touch with our Sales Manager Norman Johnson. Norman offered Arron a radio sales package, but Arron decided it was too much money to spend. Norman shook Arron's hand and left the store.

Six months after that Arron called again saying that wanted to buy some radio advertising because he was having a going out of business sale.

Arron had a great location, and a great product but he wasn't reaching out to enough people. Even though we tried to help Arron, he didn't take our advice and went out of business.

Branding is a Numbers Game

You want to get as many people as possible to know about your brand as often as reasonably possible.

The best brands are well known by millions. There are some brands that are so well known that they become the name for a whole category (Levi's, Uber, Coke).

Your goal is to get as many people as possible to know your brand because branding is a numbers game.

Branding is a Game of Strategy

Successful brands use strategies to persuade people to buy. Unsuccessful brands have no strategy and end up going out of business.

For every strategy, there are tactics.

Strategy	Tactics
Sell products on your website	Buy domain name, build site, SEO, SEM, launch site etc.
Host a product demonstration	Select venue, book venue, advertise, etc.

"Strategy is the destination and the tactics are the steps you take to get to the destination"

Think of it like this, strategy is where you're going, and the tactics are the steps you take to get to get there. Don't confuse strategy with tactics.

The Formula for Successful Branding: Reach + Recall = Response

First you must **reach** as many people in your target market.

Your target market is people who:

1. Have a use or need or desire for what you offer

2. People who have the money (budget) to buy what you offer.

Recall is where people remember your brand offers when it's time for them to make a purchase.

If you **reach** enough people and they **recall** what you offer, you'll get a **response**. The response (conversion) you get, will depend on the call to action that you ask for.

There's a Branding Funnel that makes it easy to see and remember how to focus your marketing efforts. You'll see the funnel below.

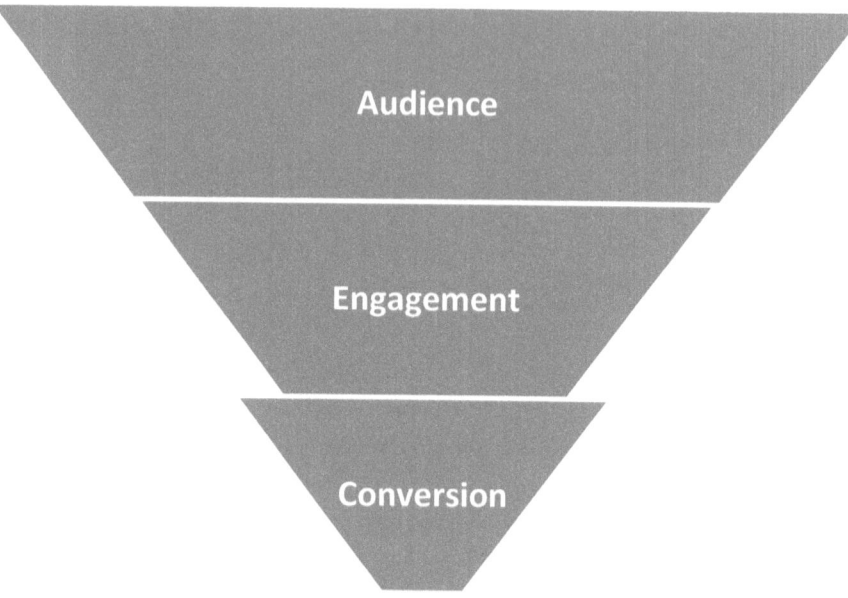

Audience: Who are you targeting? What demographics or psychographics do they have in common? You cannot brand to everyone because it is a waste of your time and money.

Engagement: This is also known as participation. Engagement begins when someone sees or hears your brand message and continues through your call to action (C.T.A.). You will learn more about your C.T.A. later in this book.

Conversion: This is the most important part of the funnel. A conversion can be as simple someone responding to your call to action or as wonderful as buying your product or service.

Now that you have an understanding of what branding is, and what branding does and the basic brand formula and brand funnel, next you'll learn the 23 Commandments of branding. Break these commandments at your own risk.

Branding Commandment #1 Know Your Target Customer

You've probably heard of the 80/20 rule. The 80/20 rule says that 80% of your sales will come from 20% of your customers.

I've been in sales and marketing since I was 16 years old. I got my first telemarketing job while my friends were flipping burgers and babysitting. Before I was an adult, I was learning why people buy.

I've sold everything from setting appointments for window and siding sellers, credit cards, family portraits and even water purification systems.

I've also done business to business sales selling ads for newspapers, radio stations and websites. I know what I'm talking about when it comes to selling stuff.

4 Types of Customers

In my years of selling, one of the most important things I've learned is that there are 4 basic types of customers; **cheap, difficult, sophisticated and affluent.**

You must know the kind of customer you want to build your brand with. Ideally, you'll want the sophisticated and or the affluent customer.

CHEAP:	SOPHISITICATED:
The cheap customer wants the best price and will respond to deals, sales and lowest price.	The sophisticated customer is usually ready to buy. They've done the research. They've checked out specifications and customer reviews. If you can

	satisfy their needs and wants, you've got a sale.
DIFFICULT: The difficult customer likes to feel like they are in control of the shopping experience. They ask irrelevant questions and make ridiculous demands. It's best to refer a difficult customer to your worst competitor.	**AFFLUENT:** The affluent customer buys what they want when they want it. They buy based on how they feel about what you're offering. Price and specifications are irrelevant to this customer.

You may want to brand to the cheap customer when you're first getting started in business or if you want to beat your competitor.

You'll want to fire your difficult customers as soon as you realize they are a difficult customer.

D.I.S.C. Your Targets

D.I.S.C. is a personality assessment tool based on psychographic study.

D.I.S.C. is broken down into the following four personalities:

- **Dominance**: **The Dominant personality is extremely competitive**. They hate to lose but love to win. They want the best of the best, even if they don't have the money. They are often independent, impatient, domineering, and they have a ready-fire-aim approach to decision making. These people are often the early adopters in part because they want bragging rights. Scarcity works well for the dominate type.

- **Influence**: **The influential personality is the fun one**. They are the type to never meet a stranger. They are warm and open to people and are generally extroverted. The influential people love to talk and are sometimes too trusting. These people buy based on how it will make them look to others. Status is a key factor in the purchase decisions. A great tactic to use on the influencer is social proof.

- **Steadiness**: **The steady personality is steady**. They take a measured and thoughtful approach to problem solving, they try to avoid conflict by being a peacemaker. They take their time when making decisions. Steady people are generally patient and undemanding. They show sympathy and loyalty for their loved ones and those they care about. A great tactic to use for the steady type is security. Demonstrate that there is little risk but high reward and you can sell them almost anything.

- **Conscientiousness**: **The conscientious personality type is a complex.** They follow the rules, they don't rock the boat, but they like to be in control all of the time. They respect structure and rules. They dislike pressure and will put off dealing with trouble until they have no other choice. The best tactic to use with the consciences is verifiable proof. You can also offer them a money back promise to help close the sale.

It's important to remember, that each D.I.S.C. type has a natural and adaptive style.

The D.I.S.C Profile will help you build your average customer profile (A.C.P.). An A.C.P. will help you figure out who is your most likely customer.

The D.IS.C. profile allows you to understand your customers basic personality so that you can develop your branding strategy accordingly. Check out the D.I.S.C. profile below.

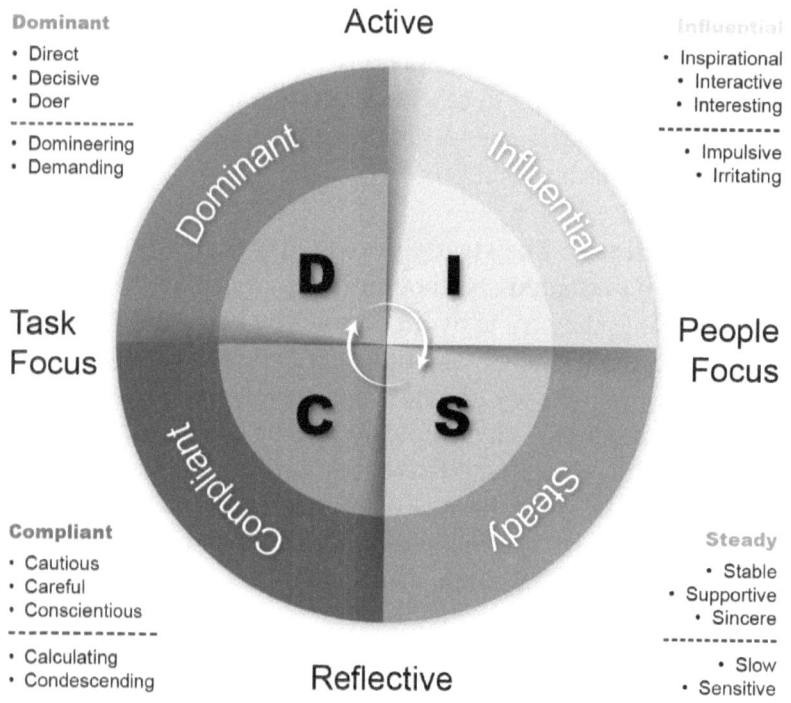

As you can see on the chart above, personalities on the left are task oriented people while the personalities on the right are people focused.

It's also important to remember that people's personalities are adaptable based on the situation. For example, a person can be very task oriented at their job but very people focused with their families. So, a person who is dominate as an employer may be steady as a parent.

They key is to know where most of your targets fall on the D.I.S.C spectrum. Remember 80% of your business will come from 20%

of your clients.

Branding Commandment #2 You Must Make Great Impressions

Whenever I coach or mentor people on marketing, I tell them to remember that *"people will treat you how they see you."*

Don't forget that branding is impression management.

Back in 2001 I went through professional sales training with the Center for Sales Strategy. There I learned that you have about 7 seconds to make a great impression. That is because human brains make a thousand computations in the first 7 seconds. In those 7 seconds, the other person is deciding if they like you or if they can trust you.

Not too long ago, while sitting in my production studio, I received an email from a client. Attached to the email was an audio recording of her vocals. She wanted to use the vocals she sent me for a radio commercial ('radio spot'). Let's call her *Ms. Belle.*

Although the copy (radio script) was good, and her voice sounded amazing, the quality of the audio wasn't good because it sounded like she recorded the audio in an empty garage.

The problem was, *Ms. Belle* was trying to launch her brand to an upscale clientele, but the audio sounded low-class.

I had to explain to *Ms. Belle* that her first impression to her audience was critical to her business success and if she didn't want to make a horrible first impression, she should come to my studio to record her vocals.

Ms. Belle agreed to come to the studio and do a professional recording of her script.

As it turns out, *Ms. Belle*s vocals sounded incredibly good! She read the script about three times and it was excellent. She suggested some music and bam! We had a good script, and a good commercial.

About a year later, *Ms. Belle* has used the successful launch of her first business to launch two more locations!

Like the old 'Head and Shoulders' commercial says, "you never get a second chance to make a great first impression".

"A brand is only as good as the impression it makes in the target's mind".

You normally dress for success at work and in life generally because you know that impressions do matter! The same is true of branding. Impressions matter.

Every day on social media, you'll see typos, and misspellings from people trying to brand their business. This is a no-no! Always proofread your branding copy – no exceptions.

Every word, image, video, audio, and webpage (including social media) is a reflection of your brand. If you think mistakes don't matter in branding you are mistaken.

The Secrets of Managing Impressions

Managing impressions is the foundation that branding is built upon. You can't build your dream home on a weak foundation, and you can't build your dream brand with bad impressions.

Impressions are the foundation on which you'll need to base your marketing.

What is the impression you get when you think of Disney? Most women I know get a little giddy thinking about Disney. When most people think of Disney, they think fun and adventure, childhood memories and of course some of their favorite movies.

Disney manages impressions masterfully for their customers as well as business partners.

While working for Cox Radio in Orlando in the early 2000's I had the pleasure of being the Creative Service Director of the Tom Joyner Affiliate Station.

Tom Joyner used to host his family reunion at Disney in Orlando, FL every year. Since Tom Joyner was already in town, he did his show live from Disney. That year, I got to work on the media promotions team with Disney to produce the local elements of the Sky-Show.

What's very pleasantly surprising is that Disney communicates in fun and informative ways. From face-to-face meetings, to email's about details or venue walk-through's, all of Disney's communications are on-brand.

First impressions matter but so do second, third, fourth and fifth impressions. Every aspect of your business is impacted by the impressions you make.

The Four Components of Impressions

As Creative Services Director, Production Director, and copy writer, I've helped Pastors, Politicians, Event Promoters, and many other professionals craft their branding message.

Through formal education, trial and error and happy accidents, I've found that to succeed in branding, you'll need to use the following four components.

1. **Impressions** getting the word into as many ears and eyes as possible.

2.	**Informing** your prospects about how your brand benefits them.
3.	**Reminding** people of the big benefits you offer.
4.	**Convincing** those you've reached and informed to give you a try.

"Not advertising to save money, is like trying to stop a watch to save time"

~ *Henry Ford, founder of Ford Motor Company*

Impressions is the act of getting into the eyes, ears, hearts and minds of as many people in your target market as possible. Remember, branding is the management of impressions. But you have to get impressions first.

As a teen, in high school, one of my first jobs was as a telemarketer at Olan Mills photography studio. My job was to cold-call people and sell photo shoots to local residents.

My goal was to get four sales per day – about one sale per hour. At first it was a struggle because I was I wasn't selling at all. I'd dial a random phone number, out of a phone book. When people would answer the phone, and I would talk about everything to anyone willing to listen on the other end of the line.

The problem was I wasn't selling! Luckily for me, my manager, Elaine was awesome! She didn't make me feel like a failure and she didn't threaten me to improve.

Elaine was a master seller and coach. She made me listen and learn how she was able to sell so well.

Elaine would dial a random number, wait for someone to answer and then do something so simple and brilliant that it almost seemed too easy!

Elaine would tell to sell. So, I decided to try what Elaine was doing... to tell to sell.

I'd dial a random number, and when someone answered the phone, I simply told them:

- Who I was
- Where I was from,
- What benefit I was offering

When someone answered the phone, told them; who I was, where I was from, and what benefit I was offering. And I became very successful at selling portraits!

You can be successful at branding and selling if you remember the Golden Rule.

Golden Rule of Branding: Tell them to sell them.

If you want to turn impressions into sales, the key is to tell them about the benefits of what you're offering. Tell your prospects who you are, what you offer, and how what you offer benefits them.

Reach as many people as you can, and you will convert more impressions into more sales.

Educating Your Prospects

In their awesome book 'Made to Stick' Chip and Dan Heath share an exercise, where someone is tapping a beat on a table and asking people if they could guess the song – no one could.

I want you to try this exercise with a friend or family member. Pick your favorite song and start tapping with your hands. Then ask the person what song you're tapping. I bet you they can't name your song. Until you tell them the song you're tapping they won't know.

The same is true with branding. You have to educate your prospects or they won't know what you're offering. As humans we question most things. Educating your targets answers the questions they may have.

No matter what business market you're in there will be a lot of competition. Part of your job is to educate people of why they should try what you offer – or your unique selling proposition U.S.P. (we will cover how to uncover your U.S.P. in detail later) .

Convincing Prospects to Try What You Offer

The third component of branding is convincing someone to try what you offer. There are many methods you can use to convince someone to try what you offer. Free trials, money back guarantees, deep discounts and more.

Reminding Your Prospects

The fourth component of branding is **reminding** your targets. We live busy lives. We have work, family, faith and other issues that we deal with daily. Your job as a brand is to get your benefits top-of-mind with your prospects before your prospects decide to make their purchase.

Think about the major advertisers that offer home improvement like; Home Depot, Lowes, Ace Hardware etc.? They are constantly reminding people that they offer the tools and supplies to improve their homes and businesses.

These advertisers know that eventually, you'll need what they offer and they see it as their job to remind you so that when you need to fix something in your home or business, you're most likely to shop with them.

You have to remind your prospects to give you a try – before they buy.

Great Copy is Critical to Successful Impressions

Copy includes the words, the media (T.V. radio, images, social media etc.).

In marketing the word's you use are technically called '*Ad Copy*' or just copy.

Copy is so critical to crafting your message, that there are professional copywriters that get paid ridiculous amounts of money to create copy that converts! Part of my current day job is writing copy.

A Copywriters job is to compose copy that "converts" words into sales. Many media sales experts consider good copy as an extra salesperson.

Copywriting is a science and everyday there's someone testing an ad, crunching data (analytics), and making the adjustments needed to make the copy convert.

Words are the most important tools that you have as a marketer. Words can make or break your business and that is why you'll now learn the secrets to how to create copy that converts.

Use the A.I.D.A. Technique

"A.I.D.A. stands for Attention, Interest, Desire, Action".

Attention: There's an old philosophical question that asks, If a tree falls in the forest and nobody sees or hears it fall, did it really fall? Of course, the tree fell, but if nobody was around, it's likely nobody cares (unless it fell on their home).

The same philosophy is true of marketing, in that if a brand launches and nobody is there to witness it doesn't matter. That is why it's so important to get your prospects attention.

Interest: getting someone to want to learn about what you're offering is very important to your marketing efforts.

You'll see and hear lot's of marketers use many methods to gain your interest. Asking questions is one of the most used techniques to get people interested in what the marketer is offering.

Desire: that urge we have to possess something is desire. Smart marketers use all sorts of techniques to build desire with their prospects. Your goal when marketing your products or services is to get people to want what you offer.

Action: You'll want to get people to do something on behalf of what your offering. Back in the day, marketers would have customers mail in their requests. Then, 800 numbers became possible. Then customers where directed to websites. These days marketers us social media to get people to like, share, re-tweet and such.

Using the A.I.D.A technique is a good way to structure your branding efforts.

Branding Commandment #3 Use Your Expertise and Authority

If you log onto YouTube, you'll see hundreds of people with thousands of video views. These people are not famous in any way. So why do these people have such large followings?

These people gain so many views and followings by using their authority.

The people I speak of provide hair and makeup tutorials. These beauty gurus have so many followers because they display their expertise.

Authority and expertise are great ways to build your brand.

So far, you've heard very little about me, but I have over 33 years branding and marketing experience. I've worked as a Creative Services Director for Fortune 500 companies, for most of my career. I've also worked on campaigns for Disney, Universal Studios, Allstate Insurance Agents, and numerous large and small businesses.

People listen to me because of my authority helping brands find success on-line on the radio, social media, TV and in print.

The great thing about having authority is that you can be authentic and real. Living in your authority will empower you avoid imposter syndrome.

In what areas are do you have authority?

Branding Commandment #4 Give them the WIIFM!

WIIFM stands for What's in it For Me.

Everyone is motivated by self-interest. Understanding your prospects self-interest will allow you to build a solid branding structure for your business.

About 2 years ago, I was working with a client on a branding campaign. He was in real-estate and claimed to help homeowners and businesses with their properties. Even better he claimed to provide his services for free! Let's call him *"Mr. Big Words"*.

The problem was *Mr. Big Words* couldn't communicate to me what his business actually did. His words had no what was in it for me (or his other prospects).

While I was writing the ad copy (advertising script) I had a hard time trying to put his benefits in words.

I asked Mr. Big Words "what do you offer."? He replied, "I provide a service that provides free brokerage offerings to homeowners and business owners" Bla. Bla. Bla! His words were going into one ear and going out of the other ear.

After about an hour, I discovered that *Mr. Big Words* main targets were people who had purchased property before.

I said, "OK…"How will your services benefit them?" He literally spoke for about 20 minutes and he still couldn't provide a WIIFM!

I was getting irritated. Mr. Big Words really wanted to brand his business and he had money he wanted to spend with my company. What was I going to do to help Mr. Big Words?

I told the real estate broker, Mr. Big Words, that he'd have to advertise the WIIFM or he would be wasting his money. After I explained to him that he was about to waste thousands of dollars, he realized how important it was to communicate the WIIFM.

It turns out he provided property sellers free appraisals. So what was in it for his customers? His WIIFM was stress-free assistance for people buying and selling property. I wrote ad copy that combined that assistance with free appraisals to create his big benefit.

"Are you buying or selling your second home? Ground Play Realty Broker's will keep you free from the stress you experienced before. Ground Play Reality offers free appraisals, and we make the buying and selling process smooth and easy. Give us a call at...Or click on our website..."

So when building your marketing campaigns you'll always give them the WIIFM.

Branding Commandment #5 Don't Forget the BIG BENEFIT

Don't forget to use your BIG BENEFIT as early as possible in your brand copy. Newspaper and magazine writers have a saying, "don't bury the lead". What they are saying is start with what is most important to your audience.

These days you have between 5 and 30 seconds to grab your audience's attention. When it comes to branding, attention doesn't build. The longer it takes to get to the BIG BENEFIT the sooner your audience will lose interest in what you offer.

Let's go back to the story of *Mr. Big Words*. *Mr. Big Words* also offered great benefits to the construction industry, but he was hiding his benefit under a bunch of big unnecessary words.

What if *Mr. Big Words* described his business by using the BIG BENEFIT? "My *company gets rid of the headaches that come with the hiring and H.R. (Human Resources) of construction and demolition workers.*"

Or they could say something like, "*Our team handles the hiring, firing, human resources and legal issues of temporary construction and demolition workers so you don't have to*"

Anyone who owns a construction company has felt the headaches that come with hiring, workers compensation, or has dealt with the threat of being sued by an employee.

By saying his BIG BENEFIT early he was able to communicate his offer in a way that was quick, clear and less likely to be ignored.

Branding Commandment #6 Never Confuse Features and Benefits

What is The Difference Between a Feature and a Benefit

- **A feature is what a product or service has.**
- **A benefit is what the product or service does.**

For example, when you buy a drill, you're not buying this really cool thing that spins really fast…you are buying the ability to get your projects done faster, and easier. As one of my sales mentors told me, "You're not buying a drill, you're buying tool to help you get the job done.

If you've ever brought any health or beauty product, you paid money for the benefit of looking better, feeling better and getting closer to your health and beauty goals.

When I was a Program Director of a Radio Station in Grand Rapids, Michigan, I was approached by a very successful land developer, who wanted to open a nightclub. Let's call him *Mr. Techno*.

Mr. Techno wanted my radio station to host his grand opening with the option of doing a live broadcast every Friday night. I loved the idea because it gave my radio station, more exposure.

We agreed on mostly everything – except for the promo copy for the grand opening. . *Mr. Techno* wanted to focus on the newly renovated dance floor and his ten thousand dollar state of the art sound system and expensive laser lights.

I disagreed with *Mr. Techno*. I told *Mr. Techno* the things he wanted to promote were **features** not benefits. I argued that people cared little about his dance floor, club lights or super fancy sound system.

I *Mr. Techno* that people would come to his club to have a good time with friends, they'd come to get a good drink at a great price, they'd come to enjoy a DJ playing their favorite songs and or maybe reasonable cover charge.

Mr. Techno disagreed with me and because he felt offended, he decided not to do the broadcast – at first. But *Mr. Techno* changed his mind after asking his bartenders what they thought he should promote. After realizing what he should be promoting he realized that people would come to his club for the benefits he offered – not the features.

Luckily, *Mr. Techno* was wise enough to get a second, third and fourth opinion. Our Friday night live broadcast was the hottest event in the city during our promotion.

Never confuse a feature with a benefit. And when you need to, find a way to explain your features as a benefit. Here's an excellent rule of thumb.

Let's go back to the idea of a drill. You go to your nearest hardware store, walk through the door and see literally thousands of tools, gadgets, nuts, bolds, lighting fixtures etc.

As you walk past the isles of stuff you don't need you finally find the drills. You start comparing the drills and come across one in your price range. The drill's description says it comes in cardboard box, has 10 different drill bits, and weighs one pound.

Now we need to turn those features into benefits.
- Cardboard box: Eco-friendly bio-degradable

Storage box. Saves on waste to help make the planet cleaner.

- 10 drill bits: Universal drill bits to make sure you have the right bit to get the job done right then.

- Weighs one pound: Lightweight drill reduces muscle and wrist strain.

Here are the best ways to sell your BIG BENEFIT.

You can focus on the outcome of what you offer. Beauty brands are masters of branding the outcome. Here are some examples; get long beautiful curls. Have age-defying skin. Reduces wrinkles in one week. Whiter teeth after one brush.

Selling the outcome is a time-tested and proven way to increase conversions of what you offer.

You can focus on the transformation of what you offer. Brands in the fitness space are amazing at selling the transformation. The other day in our break room at work, I saw a TV ad for Jenny Craig. The spokesperson was Marie Osmond. In the ad to the left of the screen was Marie wearing some jeans. On the right side of the screen Marie was wearing what appeared to be the same jeans, but the jeans were way too big.

Looking at the screen you could instantly see a visual transformation. The right side of the screen told the story.

The key to the transformation promise is to ask yourself do you want your prospect to:

- Think:

- Feel:

- Do:

- Have:

- Be:

Branding Commandment #7 Tell Them Your Why

Why are you offering your products or services, and why should anyone care?

The greatest movements in history have been great because they were able to motivate the masses by sharing their why.

America has had plenty of movements. From the founding fathers with the Revolutionary War, Women who fought for equality and the right to vote during the Suffragette Movement, The Freedom Riders during the Civil Rights Movement and other everyday people found their why – their purpose and were able to communicate it to create movements.

Why did America's founding fathers create the American Revolution? Among many things' life, liberty and the pursuit of happiness. That was their why.

Why was Susan B. Anthony able to inspire Women and Men to stand against gender inequality? Because she had a purpose that defied unjust laws that kept Women from having a right to vote.

Why was Martin Luther King Jr. able to get people to march, sit-in and be brutally attacked in support of the Civil Rights Movement? Because people believed in his dream that one day black men and white men, Jews and Gentiles – all God's children would be able to live together as brothers and sisters.

Why was Steve Jobs able to transform Apple Computer from a small nerd shop in a garage into one of the biggest and most successful businesses in history? Because, in large part Jobs' vision to create products that made people "think different".

A good why connects people to a shared belief for a better outcome in the future.

An exceptional why will connect with your followers on an emotional level. An excellent why will motivate your followers to become supporters and ambassadors of your mission.

Guy Kawasaki says in his best-selling book *Rules for Revolutionaries*, "make evangelist's not sales" when you have a compelling why, people will become evangelist's not just customers.

What is Your Unique Selling Proposition (U.S.P.)?

Your U.S.P. is the WHY that makes your products or services different or better than your competition. You must have a U.S.P. in order to win your unfair share of your market. It will be easier to find your U.S.P. once you've conducted a S.W.O.T. analysis (more on S.W.OT. later).

Your U.S.P. will help you communicate your WHY for effectively.

For example, why use the 23 Commandments of Branding? Because other branding resources only provide sales and marketing theories. This resource gives you real-world proven tactics and strategies that work.

Use your U.S.P as an opportunity to brag about your brand. Beat your chest and tell the world why your products and services make you the king or queen of the market. Bragging will fit perfectly into your U.S.P. and your WHY.

Your U.S.P. is what makes your product or service different and or better than your competition.

My U.S.P. is proven branding and marketing expertise, to help you succeed, based on over 20 years real-world experience, neuroscience, and behavioral economics.

My approach is different and better because most marketing consultants base their theory on what they think, read, heard or copied from someone else. I only provide real-world knowledge learned from years of trial and error and failure and success.

Your U.S.P. should provide you with a competitive advantage over your competition. Your U.S.P. must provide a BIG BENEFIT for your targets and prospects.

Take a moment to think about your U.S.P. then write down some ideas for your U.S.P. and then refine and perfect it as best as you can.

Testimonials Work Wonders!

Testimonials are a form of social proof. That's why you should use testimonials as often as possible. If you're the technical type, they're known as 3rd party endorsements and they work wonders. Use testimonials in your branding efforts and you will see wonderful results.

These day's 3rd party endorser's have a new name. They are called *Influencer's*. This is because every once in a while in order to stand out some ad agency takes an old concept and attempts to make it seem new by calling it something different.

It's well known that word of mouth advertising is the best form of advertising and testimonials are simply word of mouth advertising.

In 2014, I was working with a fitness trainer who wrote his own ad copy. Let's call him" *Mr. Fit*".

Mr. Fit could've been a health club model. He has strong shoulders, ripped biceps, washboard abs and muscular legs. Mr. Fit came to me because he was upset because his commercials, at that time, were not getting him any results.

To satisfy Mr. Fit and show him that doing business with my company was a wise investment, I asked him to let me help him write his ad copy. Mr. Fit agreed. On the day of the ad copy session, Mr. Fit brought a stunningly beautiful woman with him to my studio. She was only supposed to voice the new ad copy we were writing up.

This stunning woman had a firm yet feminine body with all the right curves in all the right places. I asked her "so how do you know Mr. Fit"? She eyes started to twinkle as she described how Mr. Fit found her in a depressed state, 50 pounds overweight and considering suicide.

That's when the lightbulb went off in my head! I told Mr. Fit "you should let her do a testimonial for you". We all agreed and produced a radio commercial telling the story of how Mr. Fit helped her lose 50 pounds, gain self-esteem and prevent suicide. Fast forward six months later and Mr. Fit came back to the radio station to buy more commercials because he was doing so well that he had to hire more staff!

Trust me when I say testimonials are a great way to share your WHY.

Branding Commandment #8 Sell that Sizzle

When I got my first internship in radio, I had to interview everyone at the radio station so I could better understand their jobs. One of my meetings was with salesman named George. George earned millions of dollars doing radio sales! George was about 50 years old, was in terrific shape for his age. George was winning at life, and I wanted to learn from him asap.

I remember asking George, "what makes a good salesperson"? George replied, "I don't sell the steak, I sell the sizzle". I didn't understand at the time. But over the years I realized what George meant.

When you go to a restaurant you're not just ordering food, you're ordering an experience. You're ordering the anticipation of eating something delicious; you're ordering a pleasant dining experience. Ideally, you're ordering quality service and you're ordering a delicious meal without the labor of cooking the food for yourself.

So, when you're marketing your business don't just market the products or services you offer. Go further, and market all of the physical and emotional benefits that come with your product or service.

Sell the sizzle! Sell the outcome! Sell the transformation!

In 2004, two business partners and I started one of the first ever podcasts called 'Generation Next Sports'. We needed a website to host our podcasts so we hired a guy named Marcus. We all pitched in a paid $900 each for Marcus to build our website.

We paid Marcus so much money ($2,700) not because he built websites. I started building my own websites as early as 2001. We hired Marcus because his work was exceptional, hassle-free and were supporting a friend.

We could've hired anyone to build our website, but Marcus sold us on his sizzle. Marcus sold us on having a professional website without all the hassle.

At the time we thought we got a great deal for only $2,700 (think). We felt that having a website would help us get more sponsors and it did (feel). We were able to upload our podcast segments to the website easily (do). And we had a website that we were proud of (have).

Looking back, we paid way too much for what Marcus provided. But even today I don't regret investing my $900 for a website.

If you want your brand to be successful, be like Marcus and sell the sizzle.

Branding Commandment #9 Sell Excitement

Most marketers believe that nothing sells like sex. But do you know what sells better than sex? Excitement!

One Thanksgiving my ex-girlfriend and I went to downtown Disney in Orlando, Florida to see the move *Southside with You*. After the movie we took a romantic stroll through downtown Disney. Living in Orlando, we'd been to at least 20 times including all of the parks. This time though, I noticed something I hadn't before.

What I noticed was that in downtown Disney they had exciting up-tempo music playing (from every genre you can imagine). We heard Latin Jazz, Blues, House, Soul, and Rock. The thing we noticed was that the music changed about every 50 feet.

We then noticed that kids and adults were bopping around all happy and excited. After about 30 minutes of walking around downtown Disney I was happy and excited and ready to buy something from one of the many expensive stores. My ex-girlfriend being the frugal one, grabbed me by the hand and broke me from my trance.

Excitement is infectious!

So, my question is what is exciting about your business? Not just exciting to you but exciting to your customers.

What's exciting about this book you're reading is that it contains action steps you can take today to be successful by using the power of branding! I know that the idea of your brand succeeding excites you...

So how do you make what you offer sound exciting? The answer is, once you find your BIG BENEIT making what you offer exciting will be easy.

Branding Commandment #10 Make it Easy to do Business with You

Have you ever heard of Behavioral Economics? Behavioral Economics is the Study of what makes people buy.

One thing that Behavioral Economist (Scientist who study Behavioral Economics) agree on, is that those who make doing business easy for their customers get more business.

Behavioral Economists understand the concept of 'brain-drain'. Thinking is scientifically proven to drain your brain.

There have been a few scientific studies using Functional Magnetic Resonance Imaging machines (FMRI) which show that when people are forced to think their brain uses glucose (energy) to process thinking. This thinking causes brain-drain.

Have you ever noticed that when you're under mental stress, you crave your favorite sugary or salty foods? That's brain-drain at work. Your brain wants to replace the glucose lost while you were thinking.

Why do you think most fast-food restaurant's offer only a few items? Because these restaurants have done research which has found that more choices creates a brain-drain which leads their customers to feel less satisfied after their meal.

It seems strange but Amazon.com is brilliant at making it easy to buy from them. Amazon tells you everything you'll need to know about any item you're interested in before you click add to shopping cart button.

Recently, I was in the market for a new pair of boots. I logged onto Amazon.com to see what they had to offer. I saw a range of boots. So I clicked on a pair of black boots with a zipper on the side.

What I saw in the product details for the boots impressed me. I was able to click a drop down menu to see if they had my boot size. Then I was shown the price of the boots (in my size) and then as I looked over to the right side of my screen, I saw the expected delivery date of the boots, if I purchased them that day.

Next I looked up and saw that the boots I had in mind had hundreds of customer reviews (social proof we'll get to that later) and with one click I could be wearing those boots within days. Amazon makes it easy to purchase and that is why it dominates ecommerce.

If you make doing business with you easy, you'll greatly improve your chances of having loyal customers as long as you're in business.

How can you make doing business with your company easy or easier? As you make doing business with your company easier you'll see an increase in your conversion rates.

Branding Commandment #11 Know when to use Logic and Emotions

Beware! Don't be like the majority of marketers who rely only on logic to persuade people to buy from you. There is a time to use the logical approach and a time to use the emotional approach.

Use Logic When:	Use Emotion When:
• Branding in a price competitive market	• Branding in a personal interest market (personal trainer, life coach etc.)
• When selling big ticket items (real estate, automotive etc.)	• Branding to someone who's buying for someone else (engagement rings, holiday gifts etc.)
• You are branding business to business (most times)	• When you're new to the market and you don't have a lot of credibility
• You have a good track record in your market	

The Top 6 Emotions

1. Anger
2. Disgust
3. Fear
4. Happiness
5. Sadness
6. Surprise

Every emotion has a sub-emotion. For example; anger has sub-emotions of; rage, outrage, fury, wrath, hostility, ferocity, bitterness, hate, loathing, scorn, spite, vengefulness, dislike, resentment etc.

Below you'll find a great list of emotions and their sub-emotions.

http://changingminds.org/explanations/emotions/basic%20emotions.htm

Emotions work because it's not what you say, it's what people feel.

You should find a way to use these emotions as part of your marketing efforts.

I'll admit, when I first started marketing, I thought just give people the facts and let them decide for themselves logically.

It's accepted in sales and marketing circles, that people, make decisions emotionally and justify those decisions rationally. In my experience, working with client's this is true.

Pleasure is another great emotion to help you succeed at marketing.

Publix Supermarkets has the slogan "where shopping is a pleasure". And if you've ever shopped at Publix, you know that shopping being a pleasure is more than just a marketing slogan.

One day, I was shopping for some Ezekiel Bread. I couldn't find it. I saw a Publix associate in the familiar green shirt and asked if Publix had the bread in-stock. The Publix associate said yes and walked me to the exact spot where the Ezekiel Bread was!

The sad part for me is that every time I go into Publix, I spend way more than I had budgeted. That's because at Publix, Shopping truly is a pleasure.

Remember that emotions sell very well.

"It's not what you say it's how your prospect feels".

You'll be more successful if you rely on emotion more that you rely on logic when it comes to marketing.

Humor works well for marketers because laughing makes people happy. Legendary marketer David Ogilvy, who is considered the Godfather of marketing, is known to have said, "the best ideas come from jokes".

Comedy works so well in marketing because laughter makes people happy even if only temporarily. When you can, or when appropriate, use humor in your marketing efforts because humor will help set you apart from the business crowd.

Neuro Science has found that smiling and laughing increases dopamine. Dopamine is one of the feel-good chemicals in our brains. If you can make people laugh, you'll make them happy.

.

Branding Commandment #12 Shake Them Up!

As humans we have different mental states. The main mental states are **Alpha** and **Beta**.

You are in an Alpha state when you feel comfortable like when you're watching mindless television while relaxing in your home. The Alpha state is when you mind is on auto-pilot.

Your mind goes to Beta state when you feel a threat to you or your family.

When it comes to your prospects, you want to get them out of the Alpha state and into Beta state. It's scientifically proven that people in Beta state are more engaged and responsive.

This is because of a small part of our brain called the **amygdala**, which is responsible for emotions, survival instincts, and memory.

Imagine this, you're driving down the road on a beautiful day. You've got the radio on and you're feeling great. You're in an Alpha State. Then suddenly you see a puppy run in front of your car. You grip the steering wheel and slam on the brakes. Thankfully you stop before you hit the puppy but now you are wired up. You are now in a Beta state.

When people are scrolling social media, watching TV or listening to the radio, they are generally in an Alpha state. If you want to stop the scroll or get them to pay attention to what you're offering, you'll need to get them out of Alpha and into Beta.

Pattern Interrupts

A Pattern Interrupt is an ethical way to get your target audience out of the auto-pilot to pay attention to your message. For example, memes are a great pattern interrupt because a meme can be funny, shocking or interesting.

Another example is to use relevant but unexpected brand messaging. There is a hilarious Geico commercial that features a married couple talking about how they love their home but they have a problem with Aunts. When I first heard the aunts, I though ants. Then the commercial shows the aunts in the house being critical of the married couples housekeeping abilities. It was funny relevant yet unexpected.

Neuroscience and Behavioral Economics studies find that fear of loss motivates people more than the hope of gain.

Why do advertisers say" Hurry! Limited time offer" or limit 2 per customer? Advertiser's use this because people want to avoid losses more than they want to get gains. This is known as 'loss-aversion'.

Many employees go to jobs they dislike or downright hate. Why? Because they don't want to lose the money or they don't want to be fired. Their fear of being fired and not being able to pay their bills motivates them more than the benefit of getting a paycheck.

So, when it comes to branding, you'll have to get customers out of the Alpha state and into the Beta state by using fear and risk of loss.

Make your prospects think about what they will risk or lose by not doing business with you. Also remember if you don't finish this course, your branding efforts will suffer.

Branding Commandment #13 Use Reference Points

A reference point is a comparison tactic that smart brands use in very competitive markets. For example, imagine you're walking through a store shopping for bottled water. You see a sign that says was ~~$1.49~~ now .99 cents. That is not just a discount, it's also a reference point. You instantly see that you're saving 50 cents on the same item.

You'll see reference points used in all sorts of branding, marketing and sales offers. Recently I was shopping for a new car. I found a car I liked with low miles, leather interior, moonroof and all the bells and whistles.

The car was listed at what I thought was a fair price. Then I went to Kelly Blue Book to check out the actual value of the car I had my eye on. I was shocked to see that the car dealer was trying to sell the car at $4,000 over Kelly Blue Book. That changed my reference point. I didn't buy that car.

"Reference points act as shortcuts in the buying cycle".

Great brands use reference points in all kinds of ways. Next time you see or hear an ad that promotes any percentage off (e.g. save 10%) they are using a reference point.

Infomercials are notorious for using reference points. How many times have you seen or heard something like this, "how much would you pay for this product…not $200. Not $100.for a limited time you'll only pay 3 easy payments of $33!"

You can use reference points to preserve the value of your product while helping your prospects feel like they are scoring a great deal.

__Branding Commandment #14 Appeal to Your Target's Pain__

No matter what business you're in, someone is looking for a solution. But to offer the solution you've got to find the persons pain.

At one time or another we all experience some sort of pain, mentally, physically, psychologically or emotionally. As yourself, "what problems do my prospects suffer with and how does what I offer relieve their suffering"?

Pain is relative. For instance, it's a scientific fact that women have twice as many pain-receptors as men. Despite this fact, women can generally deal with physical pain much better than men.

I'm sure you've seen a woman who has the flu taking care of everyone else in spite of her aches and pains, while a man suffering from the same strain of flu acts like he's about to die! Pain is relative to the person.

Every holiday season, people experience a phycological and emotional pain – especially children. Their pain is comes from a longing for their hearts desire for the holidays.

The desire for the latest and hottest toy, the newest fashion or that engagement ring can cause mental and emotional pain and suffering.

"You can use your prospect's pain to your advantage, but first you have to discover and uncover their pain."

So, how do you find your prospects relative pain? The answer comes back to finding your why, and then probing deeper to find their pain.

Let's do a role play? Suppose you're looking for a new car. I'll ask a few questions to discover what your pain is.

You: I'm really interested in the new Tesla.
Me: Why are you looking at that car?
You: Because these gas prices are too high.

If I'm selling cars I've just successfully uncovered your pain point – high gas prices. Based on your answer, I easily figure that since gas prices are too high, what you're paying for gas in giving you financial insecurity.

After you discover your targets why, you can then probe to find their pain points, and then you can hit them with why your product or service can relieve their pain.

Find your target's pain points and then use those points in your branding efforts.

Branding Commandment #15 Make Your Message's Stick

Making your marketing stick to the in the mind of your prospect's is easy of you use the *'SUCCESS Method'*.

The 'SUCCES Method' was developed by Chip and Dan Heath in the best- selling book, Made *to Stick: Why Some Ideas Survive and Others Die.*

S.U.C.C.E.S. stands for:

- Simple
- Unexpected
- Credible
- Concrete
- Emotional
- Stories

Simple: is just that. Simple. For example, "Save money. Live Better. Walmart." When you're pressed for time remember the words of Sales Guru Chris Lytle. "Simple is better than creative."

K.I.S.S that copy (Keep it Simple Sweetheart).

Unexpected: Using relevant yet unexpected copy breaks thought patterns and will help your copy break through the clutter.

Credible: There are several ways to establish credibility with before and after examples and client testimonials.

Concrete: Concrete details help sell by using hard facts or deadlines. For example, "for two days only, save 25% off everything in the store" or, "15 minutes could save you 15% or more on car insurance".

Emotional: There's a saying that goes, "It's not what you say, it's what people hear". I borrowed that from Pollster Dr. Frank Luntz and remixed it. "It's not what you say it's what people feel". You can never underestimate the power of emotions when writing copy.

Stories: Stories sell by engaging the listener or reader and taking them along on a journey. As I type this I can see the white background on my screen, and imagine the clicking and clacking of my keyboard.

The subject of stories needs a little more attention. I recently heard the legendary movie director Ron Howard say that there are 7 basic stories that people tell.

7 Basic Storylines

1. Overcoming the Monster.
2. Rags to Riches.
3. The Quest.
4. Voyage and Return.
5. Comedy.
6. Tragedy.
7. Rebirth.

Overcoming the Monster is the classic Davis vs. Goliath story. The plot of this storyline is how someone faced impossible odds against a bigger challenger, or a system stacked against them, yet they prevailed and succeeded.

Rags to Riches is the plot where someone started from nothing yet overcame adversity to become a success.

The Quest plotline involves the quest for riches or adventure and the temptations and setbacks along the way.

Voyage and Return is where a character goes away and returns with knowledge, or enlightenment or a good story to tell.

Comedy is a funny story told to amuse or entertain people.

Tragedy stories usually have a moral at the end. Normally in a tragic story the main characters are suffer some great loss due to an error on their part, or due to bad luck.

Rebirth is the plotline where someone deals with difficulties but somehow finds the inspiration to learn from their mistakes, change their ways and become a better person from the experience.

Using one of the 7 storylines will allow you to connect with your audience when you're branding your business. Stories allow you to write compelling brand copy, make excellent blog post's and use for customer testimonials.

Branding Commandment #16 Know How to Beat Your Competition

No matter what business you're in, there will be competition. You have to take competition very seriously or else your business can fail.

Competitive analysis is where you can have an advantage. There's an easy way to assess the competition that's used by the major marketers.

The S.W.O.T. Analysis

S.W.O.T. stands for strengths, weaknesses, opportunities, threats. This analysis will help you brand your business against the competition through careful analysis.

STRENGHTS	WEAKNESSES
OPPORTUNITIES	THREATS

Take some time to do a SWOT analysis on your business and then do another on your five nearest competitors. Be honest with yourself.

Halo's vs. Horn's

Halo vs. Horns Effect

We all have cognitive (mental) biases. These biases make us think some people are better or worse than others. One of the most notable cognitive biases is *'the halo effect'*.

People are influenced by the halo effect in more ways than we'd like to believe. For example, when we see a person dressed in business clothes we tend to think this person is respectable, successful, and of high morals. On the flip-side, when we see someone dressed like a homeless person, we tend to think they are lazy, crazy or both.

In 2007, Prof. Emily Pronin of Princeton University did a research study in which she showed the same man shown pictured differently. In the first picture she showed the man dressed like a bum and in the second picture she showed the same man dressed in a suit.

Professor Pronin gave her participants $1,000 to invest and then asked how much money they were willing to invest with each person based on their competence.

It turns out that the man in the suit was judged more competent (halo) and received $535. The man dressed casually (horns) only received $352 and was judged as untrustworthy.

So, how can you use the halo vs. horns strategy in your branding efforts? Give your business the halo and give your competition the horns.

You see the halo vs. horns tactic used in political adds all the time. People claim that they hate negative ads but it they work. In politics they call giving the opponent horns "driving up the negatives" on the opponent.

The key is to give to brand your business with halos and brand the competition with horns.

Branding Commandment #17: Create Copy that Converts

Copy is advertising speak for the words you use to get your message across. Copy is known by a few different names like; script, ad, and content.

When it comes to building your brand, copy is king. Make no mistake, copy can make or break your brand. Remember this, great copy sells but bad copy fails.

"Great copy sells but bad copy fails"

In this section, you'll learn my proven methods for writing copy that converts targets into customers.

Writing copy that converts requires understanding of the process. Copyrighting is a process that combines art, science and intelligence. The artistic part is writing copy that appeals to your targets tastes. The science part is using the words and techniques that get your targets to comply with your call to action. The intelligence part is using data and insights to see how to modify your copy for better results.

Over the last 33 plus years I've written copy for many businesses and what I've found is that great copy comes down to the 3 N's.

The 3 N's: Negatives, Names, Numbers

Negatives: When I was programming my first radio station, my news director said, when it comes to news "if it bleeds it leads". Think about the news stories you see or hear at the top of the newscast? Those stories are always about murders, robberies, war and other horrific things that humans do to one another. Have you ever wondered why?

Negativity makes people pay attention (getting them out of Alpha Mode and into Beta Mode). In psychology, this is known as Negativity Bias or Negativity effect. Studies have shown that negativity increases attention, thinking, learning and memory more so than positivity does.

It's counter-intuitive because if you ask people, they will claim they are positive. Negativity also goes back to loss aversion (people fear a loss more than they hope for gain).

So, how do you use negativity in your branding efforts? The easiest way is to use negative words in your copy. For example, " don't miss out on your chance" or "nobody save you more money" or "If you didn't buy from xyz you paid too much".

Using negatives is really easy once you think about it. Think of a positive statement and make it negative. Below is a quick exercise to show you how easy it is to make a positive statement into a negative one.

Positive Statement	Negative Statement
"They say that clothes can make a great impression."	"They say that bad clothes can break a break a great impression"
"More people use XYZ brand to save more money "	"People who didn't use XYZ brand to save more money regretted their decision later"

Negative statements work great with headlines, blog post's, social media graphics as well as in radio and TV copy. The easy way to create negative copy is to put a negative word in your statement.

Names work because as humans we all seek to connect with people in our own way. I know names work because in my internet marketing efforts I've found that when I use names in blog posts or other materials, the client engagement is much higher than when I didn't use any names.

For example, If you heard the lead singer of R and B group made a new song, it wouldn't be as compelling as if I said, Beyonce made a new song.

Names are effective in headlines and for branding because the increase engagement and involvement.

Numbers are effective because they are concrete and can help amplify your brands message. For example you can increase engagement with your brand by 80% if you use numbers with your branding message.

Have you ever noticed that the popular magazines use numbers on their covers? Men's magazines use headlines like "10 ways men over 40 can lose belly fat". Women's magazines use headlines like "10 ways women over 40 can lose belly fat".

Magazine publishers use numbers in headlines because they work. Numbers command attention. Numbers are concrete and are easy to remember.

Branding Commandment #18: Avoid Big Words

I was talking to a good friend and business owner, and she told me about a confusing encounter she had at a business networking function.

Coretta asked that all the attendee's introduce themselves. One of the attendee's (*Mr. Big Words again*) introduced himself, and started describing what his business did. *Mr. Big Words* said something like, " I provide logistical services for the acquisition of demolition and construction professionals" Bla. Bla. Bla.

The good thing about Coretta's networking functions is that she encourages all of the attendee's to provide instant constructive – and sometimes critical feedback. All of the attendees agreed that *Mr. Big Words* was using too many confusing and big words to describe his services.

It turns out *Mr. Big Words* provided temporary construction workers for construction and demolition projects.

Avoid using big words when small words will work better.

Branding Commandment #19 Don't forget Your Call to Action!

"Log on now". "Don't miss your chance". "Call toll free 800-555-5555". Those are 3 examples of a call to action.

Many brand experts waste their time creating copy, broadcasting it to the world and forget the call to action. Every aspect of your brand efforts should have a call to action (C.T.A.).

Every brand must have a call to action. A call to action can be as simple as a link saying "learn more" or "hit like".

A call to action is simple but critical to building your brand. So you don't screw up your call to action, keep it simple. Don't get too wordy with your call to action. Tell your prospects what you want them to do in a straightforward way. AVOID getting cute with your CTA. Keep your call to action simple and straightforward.

Branding Commandment #20 Use a Swipe File

"The good artist borrows but the great artist's steals"
~ Quincy Jones ~

A swipe file is a collection of headlines and copy that copywriters use to steal great ideas from others. It's been said that there are no new ideas under the sun. This is true when it comes to branding.

If you see a good idea I urge you to steal it. But please don't plagiarize if you use another person's work or idea make sure to give them credit.

A swipe file gives you idea's to use if and when you get writers block. Some of the greatest idea's you can swipe come from outside your field of expertise. Don't be afraid to look for ideas outside of your business category. Always keep your eyes and ears open for great swipe ideas.

The key to a swipe file is to keep that file somewhere handy, so you can grab those swiped ideas and use them when needed.

Branding Commandment #21 Brand to the Media You're Using

A big mistake that many people make when trying to brand, is not properly branding to the media they are using. For example, if you're using video marketing you can't write your copy the same as you would for radio, or the internet.

For example, say you've got a great headline, let's say "20 can't lose reasons to buy from xyz online" and you plan to use it in a TV ad, most people are not going to listen to all 20 of your reasons let alone remember all 20.

Some media is time-bound. Radio and TV commercials have a maximum time of 60 seconds. Sure, there are infomercials that you can use for T.V. and radio but I'm skeptical on the effectiveness of infomercials for branding. Keeping in mind your time restrictions will help you focus and create your brand copy to be more effective.

If you're using graphics (flyers, brochures etc.) you cannot use wordy copy because you're space-bound. You can't put everything you want on a flyer.

Social Media allows you to write long copy but the attention span on social media is notoriously short. In fact, if you use any more than 250 words in your social media post's engagement will suffer at the minimum and at worst, you'll lose followers.

Keep your social media posts short and drive them to your website if you have more information to share.

Your best bet for long copy is to place that copy on your website. Long copy is effective on websites because it allows you to tell your story no matter how long it is. Make sure you keep in mind the media (medium) you're branding on.

Branding Commandment #22 Use A/B Testing

Once you've written what you believe is great copy test it against other variations of that copy. Brand masters call this testing A/B testing. It's easy to do an A/B test.

First, create your first brand message (message A). Then create a variation or totally different at (message B). Then you'll check your analytics (clicks) to see which message has the best engagement.

Branding Commandment #23 Be Consistent

Consistency is key to successful branding. There's an old cowboy saying, "you don't change horses midstream". There's another saying I like, "leave with the one who brought you to the dance".

Once you find out what works brand wise, keep doing what works or you face the risk of losing market share. There are many companies that stopped doing what works and lost market share.

Remember the dude you're getting a Dell guy? Rumor has it that he was caught smoking weed so rumor has it they fired him. I think that Dell made a major mistake. Dell computers were almost a verb.

I dare say Wal Mart made a mistake when they changed their slogan from "always low prices…always". Wal Mart is still a giant of a brand but the company has taken some public relations hit's after they changed their slogan to "save money, live better".

In my educated opinion, once they focused on living better people started to question how Wal Mart pays and treats their employees.

It's not only important to keep your brand consistent, it's also critical that you keep branding through advertising.

As a rule, on average, it takes 6 weeks to see the results of your branding efforts. Once you stop advertising, it only takes about two weeks to lose your brand share.

These are the 23 commandments of branding. Break these commandments at your own risk. But if you use these commandments in your branding efforts you'll see your efforts produce results you'll be proud of.

All the best of branding success!

Sincerely,

Jerome Ford.

About the Author:

Jerome Ford is a has been in sales and marketing since he was old enough to legally work. He has successfully helped clients in nearly every business successfully brand and market their businesses.

Jerome is a master of SEO, SEM, website building and social media marketing.

Jerome currently works full-time in Multi-media in Charlotte NC.

If you found value in this book, please leave me a review?

Thank you for reading!

www.ingramcontent.com/pod-product-compliance
Lightning Source LLC
Chambersburg PA
CBHW031544210526
45464CB00003B/1139